Interiors *in* White

ROCKPORT
PUBLISHERS

ROCKPORT PUBLISHERS
GLOUCESTER, MASSACHUSETTS

First published in the United States of America by:
Rockport Publishers, Inc.
33 Commercial Street
Gloucester, Massachusetts 01930-5089
Telephone: (978) 282-9590
Facsimile: (978) 283-2742

Distributed to the book trade and art trade in the United States by:
North Light Books, an imprint of
F & W Publications
1507 Dana Avenue
Cincinnati, Ohio 45207
Telephone: (800) 289-0963

Other Distribution by:
Rockport Publishers, Inc.
Gloucester, Massachusetts 01930-5089

ISBN 1-56496-443-4

10 9 8 7 6 5 4 3 2 1

Designer: Karen Rappaport
Cover Image: Interior Design by Bierly-Drake Associates
            Photography by Sam Gray

Printed in Hong Kong by Midas Printing Limited.

For more beautiful work by the designers and photographers featured in this collection, please see:

Showcase of Interior Design: Eastern Edition 1
Showcase of Interior Design: Eastern Edition 2
Showcase of Interior Design: Eastern Edition 3
Showcase of Interior Design: Midwest Edition 1
Showcase of Interior Design: Midwest Edition 2
Showcase of Interior Design: Pacific Edition 1
Showcase of Interior Design: Pacific Edition 2
Showcase of Interior Design: Southern Edition 1
Showcase of Interior Design: Southern Edition 2
Colors for Living: Bedrooms by Carol Meredith
Colors for Living: Living Rooms by Jennie Pugh
Eclectic Style in Interior Design by Carol Meredith

White, by definition, is the combination of all colors. That is why, perhaps, it is the best complement to every color imaginable. White will stay cool and bright, both day and night. The clean, crisp feeling of a white room is unmatched by any other color. White is chameleon-like because of its reflective properties: It shines on its own, or can reflect other color in the room to create a soft, colored glow. It is the perfect background for showcasing a prize piece of art, a stunning couch, an intricately patterned rug. White recedes and allows architectural elements to hold their own instead of competing with color. Not only the perfect background, it is the perfect accent. Add white accents to a room full of color so that the eyes can rest. It can help create a soft, weathered look that is inviting. The classic pairing of white and black in a room with add drama to any room. From cool white linen in a bedroom to soft, cloud-like couches in a living room, white can be found everywhere in the home.

The books on the table read:
GARDENS OF FRANCE
INTERIOR VISIONS
GREAT GARDENS OF BRITAIN
Visions of Paradise
GREAT GARDENS

(above) The unifying elements of cherry and limestone create a "furniture" look for this round kitchen and adjacent family room. The down-filled banquette, cherry drink ledge, custom table (with one side open for remotes), and a collection of antique photos make this a warm and inviting center for relaxed living.

INTERIOR DESIGN

Gandy/Peace, Inc.

(left and below) INTERIOR DESIGN

Robert Stilin, Inc.

(above) Texture is the key word in this comfortable, but subtle, informal living space. Diverse fabrics complement the sisal flooring and underscore the richness of the antique Chinese bamboo underwear, which is mounted on a custom cherry rod with bronze finials.

INTERIOR DESIGN
Gandy/Peace, Inc.

(right) Stones found on the homeowner's property inspired the color palette in this comfortable space.

INTERIOR DESIGN
Gail Adams Interiors Ltd.

(above) INTERIOR DESIGN

Robert Stilin, Inc.

(above) INTERIOR DESIGN

Environmental Images by Marilyn Lundy

(right) This living room features a light hand-rubbed finish breakfront with a shell motif pediment. The breakfront provides a focal point for the conversation group of soft seating pieces upholstered in light pastels accentuating the bright, casually elegant appearance of the house.

INTERIOR DESIGN

Pedlar's Village Interior Designs

(above) INTERIOR DESIGN

VanTosh & Associates

Photo: Mike Moreland
Reprinted from Better Homes &
Gardens.® Special Interest
Publications Home Plan Ideas
magazine © Meredith
Corpoation 1992. All rights
reserved.

(left) The great outdoors comes inside through this garden-room addition.

INTERIOR DESIGN

Fran Murphy & Associates

(above) INTERIOR DESIGN

Mark Weaver & Associates

(right) A stunning gold-leaf coffered ceiling is the centerpiece of this transitional living room.

INTERIOR DESIGN

Designworks Creative Partnership, Ltd.

(below) Beige chenille upholstery and
iron floor lamps with parchment shades
contribute to the casual elegance of a
Malibu living room.

INTERIOR DESIGN
Ron Wilson Designer

(above) Custom furniture designs for sofa, chairs, coffee tables, end tables, wood screen and projection chandelier. Custom fabric treatments on columns, custom light trough, custom modular wall finish. (Custom furniture fabrication by Barry Salechian)

INTERIOR DESIGN
Michael C. F. Chan & Associates, Inc.

(above) Off-white furnishings contrast with
dark tables and the pinao in the background
to achieve a look of casual elegance.

INTERIOR DESIGN

Kuckly Associates, Inc.

(above) INTERIOR DESIGN

Ruth Livingston Interior Design

Photo: Dennis Anderson

(above) Responding to the client's taste—which favored a neutral, "timeless" palette—the designer used clean-lined, classic upholstered pieces with a mix of oriental fabrics and ethnic accessories.

INTERIOR DESIGN
Walker Design Group

(left) Sharp contrast and eclectic design elements intensify a grand entry and living room.

INTERIOR DESIGN
Designworks Creative Partnership, Ltd.

(right) Contemporary elegance permeates this president's office. The desk is crafted of Carpathian elm burl.

(below) Antique accents and contemporary art provide numerous focal points in this divided living room.

INTERIOR DESIGN

Designworks Creative Partnership, Ltd.

(above) A sensuous textural delight provided
by hand-woven casement draperies, along
with silks, leather, tapestry, marble, wood, steel
and glass, gives this bachelor's living room a
strong sense of individual style.

INTERIOR DESIGN
Pedlar's Village Interior Design

(above) INTERIOR DESIGN

M. L. Slovack Design, Inc.

(right) A massive antique pool table with inlaid and carved detailing provides visual ballast in an open-concept house with soaring volumes of space.

INTERIOR DESIGN

Rita St. Clair

Photo: Deborah Mazzoleni

(left and above) INTERIOR DESIGN

Est Est, Inc.

(left) Photo: Mark Boisclair

(above) Photo: Tony Hernandez

(above) INTERIOR DESIGN

Gail Adams Interiors Ltd.

Photo: Mark Boisclair

(right) Green and white slipcovers
help create an expression of summer
in this seasonal living room.

INTERIOR DESIGN

Ron Hefler

(above) INTERIOR DESIGN

Carol Conway Design Associates

Photo: Mark Boisclair

(above) The Oriental screen and black-and-white striped Empire-style chairs from Spain are in perfect accord with the neutral color scheme, which is a constant in this high-rise condominium.

INTERIOR DESIGN
Lloy Hack Associates

Photo: Steve Rosenthal

(above) Residence at Williams Island.

INTERIOR DESIGN

JoyCe Stolberg Interiors, Inc.

(above) Comfortable seating and tapestry fabrics create an environment of casual living enhanced further by the rusty-red textured coffee table. Note how honey tones and washed wood mix in the entertainment center.

INTERIOR DESIGN

Pat Stotler Interiors, Inc.

(this page) INTERIOR DESIGN

In-Site Design Group Inc.

(above) A fireplace defines the space,
while custom shelving gives variety and
texture to the walls.

INTERIOR DESIGN

Michael C. F. Chan & Associates, Inc.

(above) INTERIOR DESIGN

Arlene Semel & Associates, Inc.

(right) INTERIOR DESIGN

Douglas Associates, Inc.

Photo: Mark Sinclair

(above) Sparkling white and subtle gray add to
the expansive feeling of this lofty architecture.
Glistening brass and glass work well with the
block patterned fabric and contemporary art. The
impact is heightened by the informally balanced
draperies.

INTERIOR DESIGN

Linda Glantz Interiors Ltd.

(above) Provides intimate areas to allow
entertaining for one couple or seventy people.
The room centers around the fireplace but also
provides for a built-in service bar, game area,
and second conversation area.

INTERIOR DESIGN
Peter Charles Interiors

(above) Vibrant, rich colors
provide a beautiful contrast
to a contemporary, neutral
background.

INTERIOR DESIGN
Gail Adams Interiors Ltd.

(left) INTERIOR DESIGN
Carol Conway Design Associates

Photo: Mark Boisclair

(above) Designed for a professional football player, this casual media room features a custom video cabinet with room for showcasing helmets from current and former teams.

INTERIOR DESIGN
Gail Adams Interiors Ltd.

(right) INTERIOR DESIGN
Gail Adams Interiors Ltd

(right) INTERIOR DESIGN

Lowrance Interiors, Inc.

(right) In this setting, the signature element comes as a pair—two dramatic, asymmetrical chairs that carry the room's design.

INTERIOR DESIGN

Vince Lattuca, Visconti and Company

Photo: Bill Rothschild

(above) Artwork and fabrics in this contemporary living room rely on the rich palette of the Southwest.

INTERIOR DESIGN
Gail Adams Interiors Ltd.

(right) Soaring above the room, a mirror with classical themes gains prominence through its placement.

INTERIOR DESIGN
Bierly-Drake Associates

Photo: Sam Gray

(above) A careful mix of antiques characterizes this 1920s Spanish home. Highlights include the antique English Bible box next to the chair and an old English coffer is used as an end table.

INTERIOR DESIGN
Carol Wolk Interiors Ltd.

(right) Vanilla-colored silk sofas and down-filled chairs face an iron cocktail table displaying brushed pewter candlesticks and an Italian porcelain swan.

INTERIOR DESIGN
Pat Stotler Interiors Inc.

(left) The bedroom was designed for the ASID Phoenix Showcase house. The setting was a newly constructed "sixteenth century French chateau" with a view overlooking a pond.

INTERIOR DESIGN

Walker Design Group

(opposite page) A limestone fireplace and inviting overstuffed furniture complement the neutral background in a Bel-Air living room.

INTERIOR DESIGN

Ron Wilson Designer

(above) Understated elegance is achieved with gleaming white floors and walls that enhance the owner's colorful art and glass collection.

INTERIOR DESIGN
Carrie Brockman's Design Group

(right) INTERIOR DESIGN
Lowrance Interiors, Inc.

(above) In an elegant hall of a contemporary residence, each furnishing item is surrounded by ample space. As a result, antiques as well as whimsical new art furniture take on the commanding quality of objects in a gallery.

INTERIOR ARCHITECTURE
Olson Lewis & Dioli Architects

Photo: Eric Roth

(left) Timeless accessories bring a serene quality to a setting that celebrates the natural environment.

INTERIOR DESIGN
Sistine Interiors

(above) A greenhouse "folly," abundant in architectural details and exotic furnishings. Built off site and hoisted to the 8th floor terrace of a New York City brownstone.

INTERIOR DESIGN

Barbara Ostrom Associates, Inc.

An eclectic mix of periods and ideas that range from a drop-leaf table found at a yard sale to a hand-woven linen rug creates a comfortable and inviting living room.

INTERIOR DESIGN
Vicente Wolf Associates

(above) INTERIOR DESIGN

James R. Irving, ASID

(above) INTERIOR DESIGN

Lowrance Interiors, Inc.

(above) INTERIOR DESIGN

Arlene Semel & Associates, Inc.

(right) Careful manipulation of fabric
textures and finishes helps achieve
the aesthetic and functional needs of
this family room.

INTERIOR DESIGN

Interior Designs by Daphne Weiss, Inc.

(above) INTERIOR DESIGN

Blair Design Associates, Inc.

(above) Bright white cabinetry, brass drawer
pulls, and checkerboard tiles keep things light
and airy in this diminutive 12 foot x 12 foot
(3.6 meter x 3.6 meter) country kitchen.

INTERIOR DESIGN

Diane Alpern Kovacs Interior Design, Inc.

(above) INTERIOR DESIGN

Ruth Livingston Interior Design

Photo: John Vaughan

(above) The dining room is enhanced by
silver leaf, a detail that creates a light,
reflecting ambience suitable for both day
and evening entertaining.

INTERIOR DESIGN

Justin Sancho Interior Design, Ltd.

(right) INTERIOR DESIGN

Leslie Jones, Inc.

(above) The magnificent base of the dining room table brings a distinct Oriental flavor to this residence. The chairs are in the style of Chippendale, who drew heavily on Chinese design.

INTERIOR DESIGN

Anne Tarasoff Interiors

Photo: Bill Rothschild

(above) INTERIOR DESIGN

NDM Kitchens, Inc.

(above) A 500-gallon salt water fish tank
seduces diners to linger in this contemporary
space.

INTERIOR DESIGN
Carrie Brockman's Design Group

(above) A large white paper lantern by
Swedish designer, Ingo Mauer, becomes the
centerpiece of the dining area in this contemporary California hilltop home. The neutral
color pallette is set against pure white walls,
includes pale natural linen drapery fabric,
clear beechwood furniture and natural sisal
floorcovering. With details left to a minimum,
the story for this room is about shape and the
use of pale colors.

INTERIOR DESIGN

David Dalton Associates

(above) A live-in kitchen in an 1890's ocean-front "cottage" had to be stripped down to the studs due to a previous design "makeover" in the 1970's—complete with harvest gold Formica counters and acoustical tile ceilings. The challenge: making the large state-of-the-art kitchen convenient for one chef or several—and in keeping with the period of the house.

INTERIOR DESIGN

Stedila Design Inc.

(right) INTERIOR DESIGN

Environmental Images by Marilyn Lundy

(above) The cool restraint of modern
architecture provides a quiet envelope
for antiques from various periods.
Proportion and scale are important issues
in soaring rooms, which call for large-
scale artwork and furniture.

INTERIOR ARCHITECTURE

Olson Lewis & Dioli Architects

Photo: Eric Roth

(right) A richly patterned antique
Savonnerie carpet is enhanced by the
streamlined forms and compatible tones
of the dining room furniture.

INTERIOR DESIGN

Gayle Shaw Camden

Photo: Balthazar Korab

(above) The style of the original drawings and various personal items gives definition to the soothing neutral colors of this master bedroom.

INTERIOR DESIGN
C. Weaks Interiors, Inc.

(right) Solis-Betancourt created a luxurious Adam-style backdrop in this light-filled bathroom. A custom-designed vanity, marble and steel bench, and ceiling fixture bring richness to everyday activities.

INTERIOR DESIGN
Solis-Betancourt

(above) Neutral colors and design
simplicity blend with architectural
highlights to set the mood for a
tranquil master bedroom.

INTERIOR DESIGN
Patricia Bonis Interiors, Inc.

(right) When the ceiling of a room is dark,
it is tempting to go too far toward white to
lighten the room. Here, black furniture and
doors stand out in sharp relief in an oyster
white bedroom, balancing the dark wood
ceiling.

Photo: Richard Mandelkorn

(above) This monochromatic color scheme is beautiful in its subtlety. The scheme benefits from the greens of plants and the outdoor landscape, which provide gentle contrast to the pale yellow tints.

(above) INTERIOR DESIGN

Clara Hayes Barrett Designs

(above) A freestanding wall divides the
bedroom from the dressing area by turning
a closet into an architectural element.

INTERIOR DESIGN

L.B.D.A. Design Associates, Inc.

(above) INTERIOR DESIGN

Leslie Jones, Inc.

(above) A Beautiful draped bed turns
this master bedroom into a room within
a room.

INTERIOR DESIGN

Harte-Brownlee & Associates Inc.

(right) Amid a sea of pristine white, the
owner's ebony and antique desk and
collection of art catch the eye and
become the focus of the room.

INTERIOR DESIGN

Al Evans Interiors

Photo: Dan Forer

(above) A Boisserie mirror, a Jean-Michael
Frank table with pull-out leaf, a 1950s
Boomerang table, and a modern upholstered
bed give a master bedroom timeless quality.

INTERIOR DESIGN
Vicente Wolf Associates

(above) Eight custom tile patterns lend a unique quality
to the tub, walls and sink in this teenager's bathroom.
The walls are covered in black suede, and the base
and crown moldings are accented in gold and nickel
leaf.

INTERIOR DESIGN

Kathleen Formanack & Interior Design & Construction Development
Arcadia, California

(above) The canopied bed was tailored in white cotton matelasse, with natural linen bedcovers and dust skirt. The rough hewn plank flooring is set against a natural sisal rug, juxtaposing the rough material against fragile white cottons.

INTERIOR DESIGN
Walker Design Group

(above) INTERIOR DESIGN

Leslie Jones, Inc.

Shades of off-whites in variegated
textures are combined with teak and
cane furnishings to create a sophisticated
Anglo-Indian mood in this tropical island
retreat. Dominating the room is a British
colonial-style four poster bed.

INTERIOR DESIGN
Michael de Santis

(above) Vivid colors and bold shapes
unite the custom furniture and sculptured
carpet in this contemporary bedroom.

INTERIOR DESIGN
Carrie Brockman's Design Group

Al Evans Interiors
1001 South Bayshore Drive #2902
Miami, FL 33131

Anne Tarasoff Interiors
25 Andover Road
Port Washington, NY 11050

Arlene Semel & Associates Inc.
445 N. Franklin
Chicago, IL 60610
312/644.1480
Fax: 312/644.8157
e-mail: asasemel@aol.com

Barbara Jacobs Interior Design
12340 Saratoga-Sunnyvale Rd
Saratoga, CA 95070
408/446.2225
Fax: 408/446.2607

Barbara Ostrom Associates
One International Plaza
Mahwah, NJ 07495
201/529.0444
Fax: 201/529.0449
and
55 East 87 Street
New York, NY 10128
212/465.1808

Bierly-Drake Associates
17 Arlington Street
Boston, MA 02116

Brown's Interiors, Inc.
1115 Kenilworth Avenue
Charlotte, NC 28204
704/375.2248
Fax: 704/334.0982

Carol Conway Design Associates
8242 E. Del Codena
Scottsdale, AZ 85258
602/948.1959
Fax: 602/948.1959

Carol Wolk Interiors Ltd.
340 Tudor Court
Glencoe, IL 60022
847/835.5500
Fax: 847/835.0309

Carrie Brockman's Design Group
322 North Meramec
Clayton, MO 63105
314/726.6333
Fax: 314/721.0778

Clara Hayes Barrett Designs
300 Boylston Street
Boston, MA 02116
617/426.6144
Fax: 617/426.6415

C. Weaks Interiors, Inc.
3391 Habersham Road
Atlanta, GA 30305
404/233.6040
Fax: 404/233.6043

David Dalton Associates
8687 Melrose Avenue
Los Angeles, CA 90069
310/289.6010
Fax: 310/289.6011

Designworks Creative Partnership, Ltd.
6501 Park of Commerce Blvd
Boca Raton, FL 33487
561/912.9860
Fax: 561/912.9865

Diane Alpern Kraus Interior Design Inc.
4 Main Street
Roslyn, NY 11576
516/625.0703
Fax: 516/625.8441

Douglas Associates, Inc.
2525 E. Exposition Avenue
Denver, CO 80209
303/722.6979
Fax: 303/722.9663

Environments by
Marilyn Frances Lundy
One Lincoln Plaza, Suite 305
New York, NY 10023
212/362.7057
Fax: 212/362.7057

Est Est, Inc.
7050 Main Street
Scottsdale, AZ 85251
602/946.6555
Fax: 602/423.1093

Fran Murphy & Associates
71 E. Allendale Road
Saddle River, NJ 07458
201/934.6029
Fax: 201/934.5597
e-mail: ENM2@worldnet.att.net

Gail Adams Interiors, Ltd.
110 East San Miguel
Phoenix, AZ 85012
602/274.0074
Fax: 602/274.8897

Gandy/Peace, Inc.
349 Peachtree Hills Avenue, NE
Suite C-2
Atlanta, GA 30305
404/237.8681
Fax: 404/237.6150
e-mail:
charlesgandy@mindspring.com

Gayle Shaw Camden, ASID
Grosse Pointe, MI

Harte-Brownlee &
Associates, Inc.
1691 Westcliff Drive
Newport Beach, CA 92660
714/548.9530
Fax: 714/548.9528

In-Site Design Group Inc.
3551 S. Monaco Parkway
Denver, CO 80237
303/691.9000
Fax: 303/757.6475

Interior Designs by
Daphne Weiss Inc.
PO Box 7005
Boca Raton, FL 33431
561/392.6301
Fax: 561/395.4409
e-mail: dweiss4@IBM.net

James R. Irving ASID
13901 Shaker Blvd.
Cleveland, OH 44120
216/283.1991 or
216/751.1100

Joan Spiro Interiors
PO Box 1170 OVS
Great Neck, NY 11023
516/829.9087
Fax: 516/829.1578

JoyCe Stolberg Interiors, Inc.
2205 NE 201 Street
N. Miami Beach, FL 33150
305/931.6010
Fax: 305/931.6040

Justine Sancho Interior
4827 Fairmont Avenue
Bethesda, MD 20814
301/718.8041
Fax: 301/718.3095

Kathleen Formanack & Associates
Interior Design & Construction
608 W. Lemon Avenue
Arcadia, CA 91007
626/447.9157
Fax: 626/447.3546
Kuckly Associates
506 E. 74th Street
New York, NY 10021
212/772.2228
Fax: 212/772.2130

LBDA Design Associates
30 W 26 Street
New York, NY 10010
212/645.3636
Fax: 212/645.3639

Leslie Jones, Inc.
754 N. Milwaukee Avenue
Chicago, IL 60622
312/455.1147
Fax: 312/455.1264
e-mail: LJI@interaccess.com

Linda Glantz Interiors, Ltd.
329 Main
Ames, IA 50010
515/232.3752
Fax: 515/232.7467

Lloy Hack Associates
425 Boylston Street
Boston, MA 02116

Lowrance Interiors, Inc.
707 N. Alfred Street
Los Angeles, CA 90069
213/655.9713
Fax: 213/655.0359

Mark Weaver & Associates
521 N. La Cienega Blvd.
Los Angeles, CA 90048
310/855.0400
Fax: 310/855. 0332
e-mail: weaverm310@aol.com

M. L. Slovack Design, Inc.
7610 Bryonwood
Houston, TX 77055
713/956.7240
Fax: 713/682.7184

Michael C. F. Chan
& Associates, Inc.
3550 W. 6th Street, PH
Los Angeles, CA 90020
213/283.2162
Fax: 213/283.1815
e-mail: MCFCA@earthlink.net

Michael de Santis, Inc.
1110 Second Avenue
New York, NY 10022
212/753.8871

NDM Kitchens, Inc.
204 E. 77th Street, 1E
New York, NY 10021
212/628.4629
Fax: 212/628.6738

Olson Lewis & Dioli Architects
17 Elm Street
Manchester-by-the-Sea, MA 01944

Pat Stotler Interiors
6735 East Greenway Parkway
Scottsdale, AZ 85254
602/607.1934
Fax: 602/607.1935

Patricia Bonis Interiors, Inc.
8 Fairway Court
Cresskill, NJ 07626
201/894.9082
Fax: 201/894.1266

Pedlar's Village Interior Design
3562 S. Osprey Avenue
Saratoga, FL 34239
941/955.5726
Fax: 941/366.9563

Peter Charles Associates, Ltd.
17 East Main Street
Oyster Bay, NY 11771
516/624.9276
Fax: 516/624.9367

Rita St. Clair Associates, Inc.
1009 N. Charles Street
Baltimore, MD 21201
410/752.1313
Fax: 410/752.1335

Robert Stilin, Inc.
292 South County Road
Palm Beach, FL 33480
561/832.8176
Fax: 561/832.8145
e-mail: robert stilin@worldnet.att.net
and
PO Box 4189
East Hampton, NY 11937
516/380.6542
Fax: 516/329.8932

Ron Hefler
465 South Sweetzer Avenue
Los Angeles, CA 90048
213/651.1231
Fax: 213/735.2502

Ron Wilson Designer, Inc.
1235 Tower Road
Beverly Hills, CA 90210
310/276.0666
Fax: 310/276.7291

Ruth Livingston Interior Design
74 Main Street
Tiburon, CA 94920
415/435.5264
Fax: 415/435.5361
e-mail:
rlstudio@www.ruthlivingston.com

Sistine Interiors
1359 North Beverly Drive
Beverly Hills, CA 90210
310/246.1888
Fax: 310/246.1889
e-mail: boccasi@aol.com

Solis Betancourt
1054 Potomac Street, NW
Washington, DC 20007
202/659.8734
Fax: 202/659.0035

Stedila Design
135 E. 55th Street
New York, NY 10022
212/751.4281
Fax: 212/751.6698

Walker Design Group
7125 E. 2nd Street, #103
Scottsdale, AZ 85251
602/945.1460
Fax: 602/945.1322
e-mail: lwalker@neta.com

VanTosh & Associates
1477 Spring Street
Atlanta, GA 30309
404/888.0613
Fax: 404/876.0191

Vicente Wolf Associates, Inc.
333 West 39th Street
New York, NY 10018
212/465.0590
Fax: 212/465.0639

Visconti and Company
245 E 57th Street
New York, NY 10021

~ Index ~